Deadliest Animals

On the Planet

Billy Grinslott – Kinsey Marie Books

ISBN - 9781968228736

The bulldog ant, found in Australia, is widely considered the most dangerous ant in the world, its venomous sting that can kill a human in 15 minutes. They are extremely aggressive, large, and can sting repeatedly. Bullet Ant, native to Central/South America, it has the most painful sting in the world, often described as feeling like being shot. The Maricopa Harvester Ant holds the record for the most toxic venom of any insect, found in the southern US. The Fire Ant is known for aggressive swarming and venomous, painful stings.

The Tsetse fly is the most dangerous fly in the world, causing roughly 10,000 deaths annually by transmitting the parasite Trypanosoma brucei, which causes fatal African sleeping sickness. Other dangerous flies include horseflies, known for painful bites and disease transmission, and botflies, which can cause parasitic larvae infestations. Tsetse flies are large horsefly like insects found in riverine Western and savannah central and Eastern Africa.

The deadliest tick-borne disease in the world is Rocky Mountain spotted fever, often transmitted by the American dog tick and Rocky Mountain wood tick, which can cause up to 30% mortality rate if untreated. Other highly dangerous species include the paralysis-inducing Australian paralysis tick and the Black-legged tick (carrier of Powassan virus and Lyme disease).

The mosquito is the world's most dangerous animal, causing over 1 million human deaths annually by transmitting diseases such as malaria, dengue fever, Zika, and West Nile virus. Unlike large predators, mosquitoes are deadly due to the pathogens they spread, making them the leading cause of animal-related human fatalities. While large predators are feared, the deadliest animals are small insects which kill millions annually through spreading disease and toxins. Mosquitoes are responsible for the highest number of human deaths per year, surpassing all other creatures.

Roundworms are deadly because they can cause severe complications, including fatal intestinal blockages, malnutrition, and organ damage. They migrate through the body, affecting organs like the lungs, liver, and brain. In humans, a heavy infection can cause severe abdominal pain, vomiting, and in some cases, death. Approximately 800 million to over 1 billion people worldwide are infected with roundworms annually, with the highest prevalence in tropical and subtropical regions.

Tapeworms are deadly primarily when their larvae migrate outside the intestines to form cysts in vital organs, particularly the brain, causing seizures, blindness, and fatal neurological damage. Larval cysts can also rupture, causing severe allergic reactions or in rare cases, transfer cancer cells to the host. Larvae can form cysts in the liver, lungs, or heart, growing large enough to destroy tissue and cause organ failure. Approximately 50 to 100 million people are infected with tapeworms yearly in the world. Most infections come from eating undercooked pork, beef, or contaminated food/water in areas with poor sanitation.

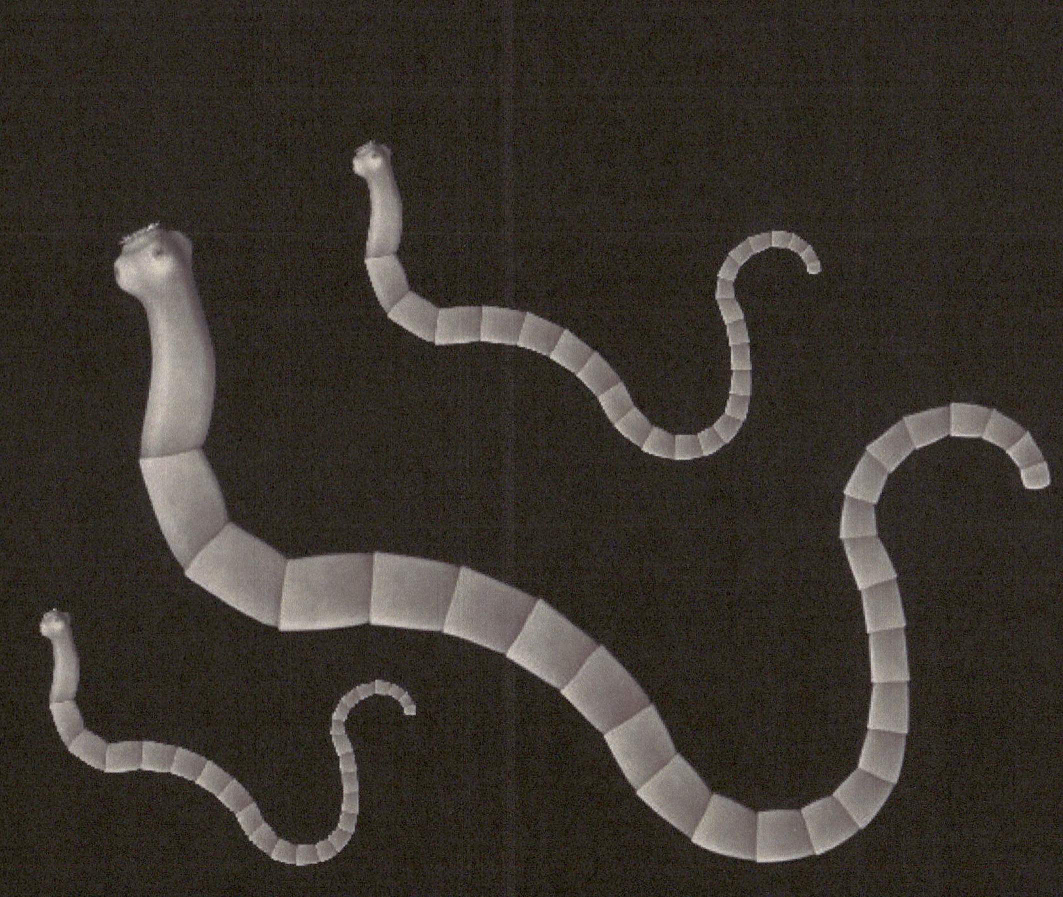

The most dangerous bee is the Africanized Honeybee ("killer bee"), known for extreme aggression, chasing victims, and attacking in massive swarms. While their venom is not more potent than others, their defensive, relentless nature makes them deadly. Africanized bees are dangerous because they swarm by the thousands and chase victims for up to 1/4 mile. Giant Asian Hornet, while technically a hornet, its massive size and potent neurotoxic venom make it one of the most dangerous hornets. They are called murder hornets, they earned their nickname for their brutal, predatory attacks on honeybee hives.

Assassin bugs are a large group of predatory insects known for their stealthy hunting, using straw-like mouthparts to inject venom and dissolve the insides of prey like beetles, flies, and caterpillars. Kissing Bugs are the only type of assassin bug that feeds on human blood, typically biting the face at night. They can carry the parasite that causes Chagas disease, a serious, potentially fatal illness.

The Deathstalker scorpion, found in North Africa and the Middle East, is widely considered the most dangerous and venomous scorpion in the world. Its highly potent neurotoxic venom can cause severe pain, respiratory failure, and death, particularly in children and the elderly. They are highly aggressive and fast, capable of moving quickly to strike. They are nocturnal ambush predators, hunting insects and small vertebrates.

The Brazilian wandering spider, often called the banana spider, is one of the world's most venomous spiders. They can have a leg span of up to 7 inches. Often ranked number one for venom potency, they are aggressive, nomadic hunters in Central/South America. Their venom is a potent neurotoxin that causes extreme pain, respiratory issues, and paralysis. Instead of fleeing, they often rear up on their hind legs and display their fangs when threatened.

Bats are a major source of rabies, causing roughly 70 percent of US rabies deaths and contributing to the 60 thousand annual global rabies fatalities. A study estimated a median of 66 thousand people in Southeast Asia are infected with SARS-related coronaviruses from bats annually. Approximately 60 thousand Americans receive preventative post-exposure prophylaxis (PEP) treatment each year for potential rabies exposure, with a significant portion resulting from direct or suspected contact with bats.

Rats cause thousands of illnesses annually, with 2 to 4 thousand cases of rat-bite fever in the U.S. Leptospirosis is a disease that is spread through rat urine, it causes over 1 million human cases globally each year, resulting in approximately 60,000 deaths annually. In the U.S., there are approximately 20 to 40 thousand rat bites each year. Over two-thirds of rat bites occur in children under 10, often resulting in bites to the hands, feet. About 10% of rat bites result in Rat-Bite Fever (RBF), which has a 13% mortality rate if untreated.

Approximately 5.4 million people are bitten by snakes annually. These bites result in 1.8 to 2.7 million cases of venomous snakebites, leading up to 138 thousand deaths and roughly 400 thousand permanent disabilities, such as blindness and amputations. Roughly one person is bitten every 10 seconds globally. The highest numbers of cases and deaths occur in Sub-Saharan Africa, Southeast Asia, and South Asia. India has the highest number of snakebite deaths, with approximately 50 thousand annually.

The most poisonous frog in the world is the Golden Poison Frog found in Colombian rainforests. It possesses enough skin-secreted batrachotoxin to kill 10-20 humans or 20,000 mice. The undisputed most toxic, these tiny frogs are roughly 2 inches long and often yellow, orange, or pale green. They are so toxic that just holding one of them can be fatal. Their poison so toxic that it can remain active on surfaces for up to a year.

Freshwater snails cause over 200,000 deaths annually and infect roughly 250 million people worldwide with schistosomiasis (snail fever). The disease, common in tropical areas, is spread when parasites from the snails penetrate the skin during water contact (swimming, washing). Parasitic worms from the snails enter the human bloodstream through the skin in contaminated freshwater. Chronic infection leads to severe organ damage, including liver damage, kidney failure, and bladder cancer.

An estimated 150 million people are stung by jellyfish worldwide each year, with incidents particularly common in the Indo-Pacific region. While many stings result in minor irritation, they can be fatal, with roughly 100 to 500 deaths attributed to jellyfish stings annually. These incidents often increase during warmer weather and beach seasons. The Australian box jellyfish is the most dangerous jellyfish, with potent venom that can kill a human in minutes.

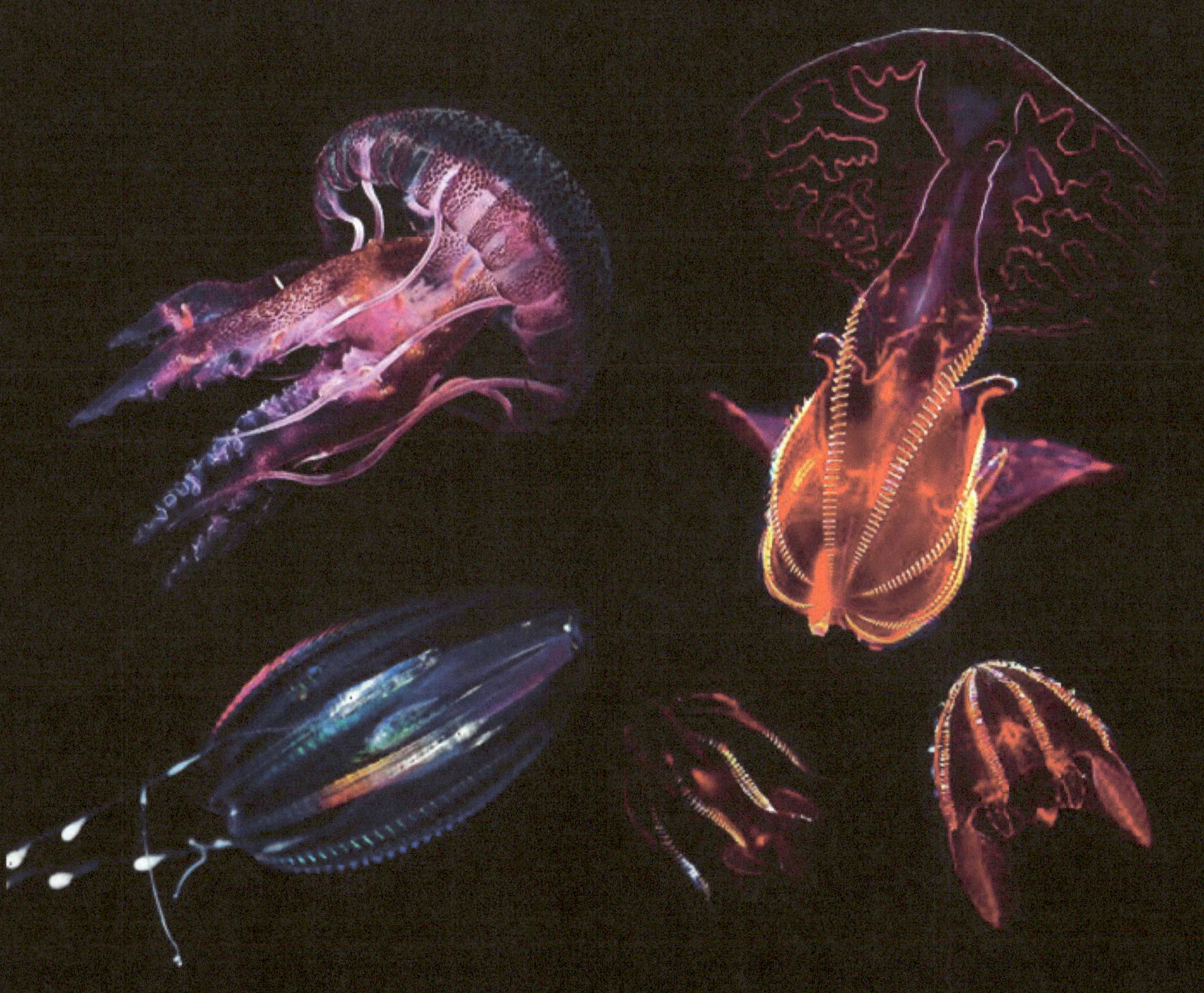

The blue-ringed octopus is extremely dangerous and, despite its small size, is one of the world's most venomous creatures. It carries tetrodotoxin, a nerve toxin 1,200+ times more potent than cyanide, capable of killing an adult in minutes. While bites are often fatal, they are rare and usually occur only if the creature is handled or provoked. One blue-ringed octopus has enough venom to kill 26 adults in just a few minutes.

Stonefish are considered the most venomous fish in the world, capable of killing an adult human in under an hour due to powerful neurotoxins released from sharp, needle-like dorsal fin spines. While not typically aggressive, stepping on them causes agonizing pain, severe swelling, necrosis, and potentially heart failure, requiring immediate medical attention. Stonefish possess dorsal spines that act as hypodermic needles, releasing potent venom when pressure is applied.

Pufferfish toxin (Tetrodotoxin) causes paralysis, resulting in difficulty breathing. There is no specific medication for treating pufferfish toxin. Tetrodotoxin is deadly, up to 1,200 times more poisonous than cyanide. One puffer fish has enough toxin to kill 30 adult humans. Pufferfish are dangerous to eat because they contain a deadly poison known as tetrodotoxin (TTX), which comes from their food.

The Great White is the most feared shark in the world. They grow up to 20 feet long and weigh up to 6,600 pounds. Great White sharks existed before dinosaurs. A Great White can eat a whole seal and won't need to eat for three months. They have 300 teeth that regrow, that's a lot of teeth. Great whites are one of the largest predatory fish on earth. The Great White, Tiger, and Bull sharks are the most dangerous to humans, responsible for the vast majority of fatal, unprovoked attacks. The Great White leads the pack, while Tiger sharks and Bull sharks follow closely.

Alligators are considered dangerous due to their status as apex ambush predators, possessing immense bite forces, extreme speed in short bursts, and the ability to camouflage in water. They can reach speeds over 20 miles per hour on land and in water, with powerful jaws designed to seize, drag, and drown prey. Alligators have one of the highest known bite forces on earth, capable of crushing bones. Alligators that have been fed by humans lose their natural fear, associating people with food, which increases the risk of attacks.

Crocodiles have incredibly powerful jaws that can crush many animals. Crocodiles have 60–110 teeth, and they can replace up to 6,000 teeth in their lifetime. Crocodiles are highly dangerous apex predators due to their stealthy ambush-based hunting style, immense bite force, and aquatic agility. They utilize explosive speed, powerful tails to strike or pull prey underwater, and the lethal "death roll" to kill their prey. Estimates suggest that roughly 1,000 people are killed by crocodiles annually worldwide. The Nile crocodile and the Saltwater crocodile are responsible for the vast majority of attacks.

Wild boars are dangerous due to their significant, muscular weight (up to several hundred pounds), speed (up to 30 miles per hour), and, most critically, their razor-sharp, self-sharpening tusks. They can cause severe injuries or death, typically targeting human legs and groin area with goring and charging behavior, particularly when threatened or protecting piglets. Weighing over 300 pounds, they can charge at 30 mph, making them difficult to escape or defend against. They can act aggressively without warning, and sometimes, if wounded, can become even more dangerous. They also carry diseases harmful to humans and pets.

The Largest Lizard on earth is the Komodo Dragon. These lizards can grow up to 10 feet long. As the world's largest lizards, adults can weigh over 150 pounds. Komodo dragons are dangerous due to their specialized hunting arsenal, which includes venomous bites that prevent blood clotting and induce shock, sharp serrated teeth, and immense size. They use a "grip and rip" attack, consuming large prey or carrion, and can run up to 15 miles per hour, making them formidable apex predators capable of attacking humans.

Ostriches are dangerous due to their immense size. They can be 9 feet tall and weigh up to 300 pounds. They can run at speeds of 43 miles per hour. They have powerful legs equipped with 4-inch, razor-sharp claws. They can deliver kicks with over 500 pounds of force, capable of killing lions and humans. Ostriches kick forward with immense power, capable of breaking bones or causing severe injuries.

Cassowaries are considered the world's most dangerous birds primarily due to their, powerful, three-toed legs capable of running 31 miles per hour, jumping 7 feet high, and delivering lethal kicks. Their most fearsome feature is a 4-to-5-inch, dagger-like claw on the inner toe of each foot, which can inflict fatal, slicing wounds. The middle toe's long, sharp, spike-like talon acts like a knife to slice, puncture, and disembowel threats. Although normally shy, they can become aggressive.

Raccoons are dangerous because they are wild, unpredictable animals that can carry deadly diseases like rabies. They pose serious health risks to humans and pets through bites, scratches, and, dangerously, their feces, which can contain parasites like roundworm. Furthermore, they are destructive, causing significant property damage by invading homes and sheds. Raccoons are a leading source of rabies exposure, with roughly 60,000 people treated for exposure annually.

Deer are considered dangerous primarily due to the high frequency of vehicle collisions. In the US, approximately 1.5 million to 2.1 million deer-vehicle collisions occur annually, resulting in roughly 440 human deaths and over 60 thousand injuries. Male deer (bucks) can become highly aggressive during mating season (autumn/winter), using their antlers and hooves to attack anything they perceive as a threat. In the US, deer are considered the deadliest animal, causing more human fatalities through collisions than bears, alligators, and sharks combined.

Moose are dangerous due to their massive size, they can weigh more than 1,500 pounds and run up to 35 miles per hour. They are highly territorial, often causing more annual injuries in regions like Alaska than bears. They are unpredictable, defensive of calves, and bulls are very aggressive during mating season. They may charge without warning, often perceiving people and pets as threats. They use their hooves to stomp and kick, which can crush bones, collapse ribs, and break limbs.

Bison are dangerous because they are massive, they can weigh up to 2 thousand pounds and run up to 35 miles per hour. They are unpredictable, capable of charging or goring people with their horns when threatened or startled. They are wild animals that can easily crush, gore, or throw humans, often causing serious injuries when people get too close. A single blow can cause extensive damage to vehicles or humans.

Sloth bears are considered one of the most aggressive large carnivore species, with attacks frequently resulting in serious injury or death, primarily due to defensive behavior. Unlike other bears that may try to flee or climb, a startled sloth bear often charges immediately, utilizing loud screams and violent, erratic attacks targeting the face. Sloth bears have poor eyesight and hearing. When startled at close range, their instinctive, defensive reaction is to attack.

Asiatic Black Bears are considered dangerous due to their aggressive, nervous temperament, combined with powerful, sharp claws for climbing and a high capability for vertical, bipedal movement. They often attack defensively when surprised or protecting cubs. In the 12-month period, a record 219 people were injured or killed by these bears.

Grizzley Bears and Brown Bears. Grizzly bears are a subspecies of the brown bear. These bears are dangerous due to their immense power and size. They weigh up to 1 thousand pounds and can be 7 to 10 feet tall when standing up. They have a bite force of 1 thousand psi. They have high intelligence, can reach speeds up to 30 mph, and have territorial instincts. They often attack defensively when surprised, protecting cubs, or guarding food, frequently returning to continue attacks.

Polar bears are considered exceptionally dangerous because they are the largest land predator and, unlike other bears, they view humans as potential prey rather than a threat to be avoided. They do not bluff when charging, if they run at you, they are going to attack. Polar bears are highly intelligent, and they possess immense strength with a bite force of 1,200 psi, designed for crushing bones. Adult males can weigh up to 1,500 pounds and stand 10 feet tall. They are incredibly fast, capable of outrunning humans, and are silent, camouflaged hunters.

Wolves are considered dangerous primarily because they are apex predators that hunt in packs, possessing immense strength, sharp teeth, and high intelligence. Wolves are carnivores capable of taking down large prey. A single adult wolf is generally stronger than a large dog. Wolves that lose their natural fear of humans due to proximity or feeding are more likely to attack. They may attack if they feel cornered, threatened, or if their dens are approached. Their social structure allows them to cooperate to bring down prey or pose a threat to livestock.

Hyenas are dangerous primarily due to their immense bite force (up to 1,100 psi), capable of crushing bone, and their highly intelligent, pack-hunting behavior. As aggressive apex predators, they possess high endurance, often attacking at night to steal food or threaten humans, especially when food is scarce. They are intelligent, coordinated pack hunters that can take down prey much larger than themselves. They are aggressive predators, often competing with lions and, in some cases, challenging them. They are known to attack, kill, and sometimes consume humans, particularly targeting children when food is scarce.

Cheetahs are deadly, highly specialized predators that reach speeds of 60 to 70 miles per hour in 3 seconds. Cheetahs are just built to kill. Not only are they fast, but they also have large forward-facing eyes that provide excellent binocular vision to see prey. They have a small head, lightweight body, enlarged heart, flexible spine, non-retractable claws for traction and massive lungs that allow for rapid oxygen intake, so they can run fast and turn quickly to attack their prey.

Leopards are exceptionally deadly predators due to their mastery of stealth, immense strength relative to their size, and their versatility as ambush hunters. They possess extraordinary, 7 times better-than-human night vision, allowing them to hunt in darkness. Their ability to haul heavy prey (sometimes up to 276 pounds) into trees, combined with their ability to hunt and ambush prey from above, makes them a uniquely elusive threat.

Tigers are supreme apex predators due to their combination of massive physical strength, specialized stealth, and a lack of fear of other animals. They utilize camouflaged, striped coats for stalking, and deliver fatal, high-pressure bites (1000-1500 psi) to the throat or neck of their prey. Other key adaptations include 3-1/2-inch canine teeth, retractable claws, and silent movement. They consume up to 75 pounds of meat in a night and can take down large prey like buffalo.

Lions are deadly apex predators due to a combination of immense physical strength, highly specialized hunting techniques, and social intelligence. Weighing up to 550 pounds, they possess crushing bite forces, sharp, retractable claws for grappling. They are unique among big cats, because they hunt in coordinated packs called prides to overpower massive prey as a group effort. Their social structure allows them to defend their territory from rivals.

Kangaroos are dangerous primarily due to their immense muscular strength, sharp claws, and powerful, disemboweling kicks. They can stand over 6 feet tall, weigh up to 200 pounds. They use their tail to stand and balance, freeing their strong hind legs to deliver devastating kicks. Their legs are equipped with large, sharp, and durable claws designed for disemboweling opponents.

The Cape Buffalo is considered one of Africa's most dangerous animals—often nicknamed the "Widowmaker" or "Black Death"—due to its unpredictable, aggressive temperament, immense 2,000-pound size, and specialized, fused horns. They are notorious for charging without warning at speeds up to 40 miles per hour, using their armor-like horn "boss" to crush, gore, and trample threats, including lions and hunters. They are highly temperamental, often charging without warning. Bulls can weigh up to 2,000 pounds and stand 5–6 feet tall, featuring a "boss" (fused, thick horns) that acts like a helmet.

Rhinoceroses are considered among the most dangerous and deadly animals in Africa. Rhinoceros are dangerous primarily due to their immense size (up to 5,000 pounds), high speeds (up to 30-40 mph), and poor eyesight, which causes them to charge defensively when threatened. While generally not aggressive unless provoked, they are highly territorial and protective. They have skin that can be up to 2 inches thick. This acts as nearly impenetrable armor, shielding internal organs from the claws and teeth of predators, so they are fearless. Rhinos have one or two horns that can grow up to 55 inches long. These horns are used as formidable weapons for goring, stabbing, and pummeling threats.

Hippos are considered the world's deadliest large land mammal, killing an estimated 500 people annually in Africa. They are exceptionally dangerous due to their extreme territorial aggression, massive size (up to 3.5 tons), and speed, both in water and on land. They often attack humans to protect their territory, using 20-inch, razor-sharp canine teeth that can easily crush predators. Hippos are fiercely protective of their aquatic habitats, often attacking boats, canoes, or people who wander too close to their riverbanks. With a bite force capable of snapping a boat or a crocodile in half, their massive, 170-degree opening jaws are used to inflict fatal, deep-piercing wounds with their sharp tusks.

Elephants are deadly due to their massive size and incredible strength. They can run up to 25 miles per hour making escape difficult and are responsible for 100–500 human deaths annually. Their aggression often stems from territorial defense, protecting young, or, in captivity, extreme stress. Weighing up to 15,000 pounds, they can easily crush, trample, or toss humans and flip vehicles. Their tusks are used for goring, while their trunks possess immense strength for throwing objects. They are particularly dangerous when protecting their calves or when they feel threatened.

Horses are considered dangerous due to their immense size, power, and instinctual "flight" response, which can lead to unpredictable, violent actions. Their ability to deliver lethal kicks, high-speed bites, and falls from great heights, makes them a significant source of injury. Globally, an estimated 1.8 million people visited emergency room departments for horse-related injuries over a 27-year period. Roughly 1 in 5, riders will experience a serious injury during their riding career.

Tens of millions of people are injured by dog bites annually worldwide, with some estimates suggesting nearly 100 million incidents, making them a significant, often underreported, global health issue. Dogs are the third deadliest creature to humans, responsible for roughly 60 thousand human rabies deaths per year. While precise global figures are hard to track, due to underreporting, dog bites account for tens of millions of injuries annually. In the US, approximately 4.5 million people are bitten annually. Roughly 1 million people in the US seek medical care for dog bites each year.

Author Page

Billy Grinslott – Kinsey Marie Books

ISBN – 9781968228736

Thanks